GUIDE TO
ARGENTINA

BOLIVIA
PARAGUAY
Salta
Iguazú Falls
Paraná River
ANDES
BRAZIL
Cordoba
Uruguay River
Aconcagua -- 22,834 ft.
Rosario
URUGUAY
Mendoza
CHILE
Buenos Aires
Río de la Plata
Pacific Ocean
PAMPAS
PATAGONIA
Mar del Plata
Atlantic Ocean
Strait of Magellan
FALKLAND ISLANDS
TIERRA DEL FUEGO
Ushuaia

ARGENTINA

MARION MORRISON

Highlights for Children

CONTENTS

On the cover: A view of snowcapped mountains and clear-blue lake in Patagonia, southern Argentina

Published by Highlights for Children
© 1996 Highlights for Children, Inc.
P.O. Box 18201
Columbus, Ohio 43218-0201

10 9 8 7 6 5 4 3
ISBN 0-87534-925-0

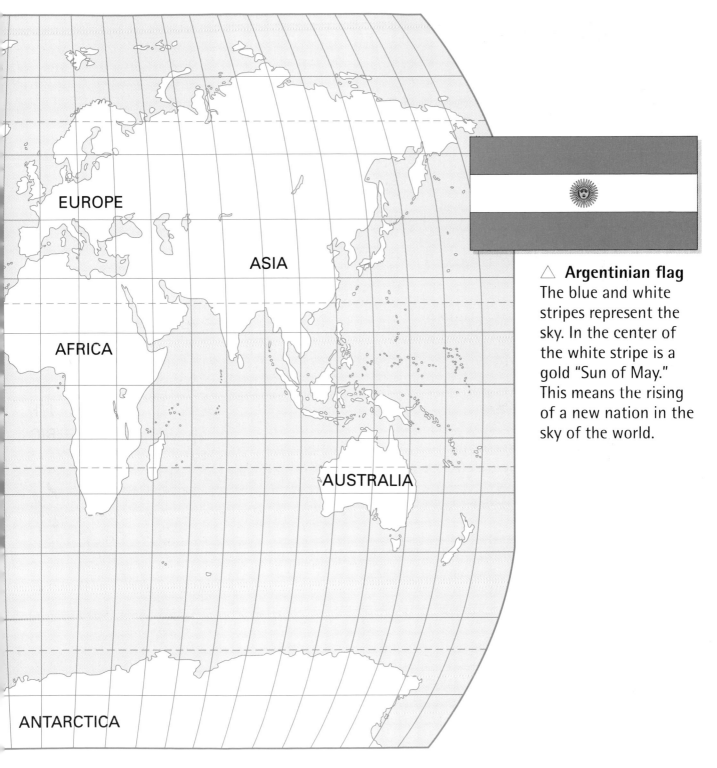

EUROPE

ASIA

AFRICA

AUSTRALIA

ANTARCTICA

△ **Argentinian flag**
The blue and white
stripes represent the
sky. In the center of
the white stripe is a
gold "Sun of May."
This means the rising
of a new nation in the
sky of the world.

ARGENTINA AT A GLANCE

Area 1,068,301 square miles (2,776,888 square kilometers)

Population 33,767,000

Capital Buenos Aires, population of city and surroundings 10,500,000

Other big cities Córdoba (population 1,148,305), Rosario (935,471), La Plata (520,647)

Highest mountain Mount Aconcagua, 22,832 feet (6,959 meters)

Longest river Paraná, 2,062 miles (3,300 kilometers)

Largest lake Lake Mar Chiquita, 810 square miles (2,074 square kilometers)

Official language Spanish

▽ **Argentinian stamps** These show national parks, plants, animals, and a Christmas scene. One shows the statue of Christ in the Andes.

▷ **Argentinian money** Argentina's currency is the peso. One peso is 100 centavos. The one-peso note shows former president Carlos Pelligrini. The back of the two-peso note shows the museum created to honor General Bartolomé Mitre, who was elected President in 1862. He is pictured on the front of the note.

4

BOLIVIA

PARAGUAY

BRAZIL

20°S
75°W   70°W   65°W   60°W   55°W   50°W

Tropic of Capricorn

25°S

A n d e s

Gran Chaco

Iguazú
Falls

Mount
Cachi ▲

San Salvador
de Jujuy
● Salta

San Miguel
de Tucumán ●

Santiago del
Estero ●

30°S

Mount
Aconcagua ▲

Córdoba ●

L. Mar
Chiquita

San Juan ●

Mendoza ●

Santa Fé ●

Rosario ●

Corrientes ●

Paraná

Uruguay

URUGUAY

Buenos Aires ★
La Plata ●

Río de la Plata

35°S

C
H
I
L
E

San
Rafael ●

Santa
Rosa ●

Pampas

Mar del Plata ●

Negro

Colorado

Bahía Blanca ●

PACIFIC OCEAN

ATLANTIC OCEAN

40°S

San Carlos de
Bariloche ●

P a t a g o n i a

Chubut

Península Valdés

N

W   E

S

45°S

Comodoro Rivadavia ●

Puerto Deseado ●

50°S

Río Gallegos ●

Falkland Islands (U.K.)

Tierra
del Fuego

Cape Horn

© Oxford Cartographers

ARGENTINA

Desert	★ Capital
Grassland & Farmland	● Major Cities
Mountains	▲ Mountain Peaks
	— Country Boundary

0   100   200   300 Miles

0   200   400 Kilometers

5

WELCOME TO ARGENTINA

Argentina is the second-largest country in South America, and the eighth largest in the world. It shares borders with five other countries — Chile, Brazil, Bolivia, Paraguay, and Uruguay. It has a long coastline formed by the Atlantic Ocean. The Andes mountain range forms its western border with Chile. This border extends 2,300 miles (3,680 kilometers) with the Pacific Ocean no more than 100 miles (160 kilometers) away.

Northern Argentina lies in the tropics and is hot and dry. The central region is mild with four distinct seasons. The far south is a frozen region of icebergs and glaciers that reach out across the sea as far as Antarctica.

▽ **Children playing in Buenos Aires** Behind them is the Congress Building.

▽ The pampas near Buenos Aires

The pampas are the vast, treeless, grassland areas of South America.

△ **Busy Buenos Aires** The streets are always full of business people and shoppers.

The land is very varied. To the north are the dry Chaco forests and the swampy lands of Mesopotamia. In the center are the *pampas*. These flat grasslands are home to cowboys called *gauchos* and to millions of cattle. In the northwest there are deserts and tropical forests. The vast windy plains of Patagonia cover the southern part of the country.

Buenos Aires, Argentina's capital, lies on the south bank of the Plate River. Other big rivers flow hundreds of miles from the neighboring countries into the Plate. The Plate River and Argentina itself take their names from Spanish and Latin words meaning "silver" because the first explorers expected to find silver.

Most of Argentina's native Indians disappeared after the Spaniards arrived more than 400 years ago. Today the people of Argentina are of mixed origins. Many are descended from settlers who arrived within the last 200 years.

BUENOS AIRES

Buenos Aires is Argentina's capital and largest city. Once it was a small port where people made a living by trading and smuggling. Later it grew into a big Spanish colonial town. Toward the end of the 1800s, many buildings and parks were built. Buenos Aires became a beautiful city known as "the Paris of Latin America." Today more than ten million people — one in three of all Argentinians — live in and around the city. They are known as *los porteños*, or "the people of the port," and the city is divided into *barrios*, or neighborhoods. La Recoleta with its famous cemetery, and La Boca, the Italian port area, are two well-known neighborhoods.

A sightseeing tour downtown in the heart of the city will take you to Plaza de Mayo and the Casa Rosada, or "Pink House," which is the president's palace. The Metropolitan Cathedral and the Cabildo are also on the Plaza. The Cabildo is the place where Argentina's independence from Spain was plotted nearly 200 years ago. It is now a museum. The long, wide Avenida de Mayo leads from the Plaza to the National Congress building. On your way there you can stop at one of the many grand, old-style cafés, or at an outdoor café on the sidewalk. The Avenida 9 de Julio crosses the Avenida de Mayo. On this busy avenue you will see a tall obelisk, or stone tower. It was built in 1936 to celebrate the four hundredth anniversary of the founding of the city.

Nearby is Calle Florida, a modern shopping street that is closed to traffic. Lively Lavalle and Corrientes streets are nearby. At night crowds of people visit the movies, theaters, bookshops, and *parrillas*, or steak restaurants. The Colón Theater, by the Avenida 9 de Julio, is famous for its concerts and its opera and ballet performances.

▷ **Avenida 9 de Julio** This is said to be the widest avenue in the world.

8

◁ **Brightly painted homes in La Boca** The famous Argentinian soccer player Diego Maradona plays for the local soccer team, Boca Juniors.

▷ **Dancing the tango** The tango, often considered to be Argentina's national dance, was made famous by singer Carlos Gardel in the 1930s.

LAND OF THE GAUCHO

Vast, flat pampas stretch north, west, and south of Buenos Aires. Travel south along the coast to Mar del Plata. Visit the city of La Plata along the way.

The seasons in Argentina are opposite of the seasons in the United States and the rest of the Northern Hemisphere. During Argentina's summer — from December to March — about two million visitors come to Mar del Plata, known as "the Pearl of the Atlantic." It is Argentina's favorite resort. It is famous for its casino, and many wealthy porteños have vacation homes here.

Another short journey from Buenos Aires is to Luján. It is a religious center and is visited every year by many thousands of devout Catholics.

As you travel across the pampas, you will see that the land is flat in all directions. There are few trees or rivers. Wind-driven and electric pumps are used to draw water from under the ground. The pampas are called *humid* and *dry* because more rain falls in the east than in the west. A variety of crops are grown on the fertile soil of the humid pampas.

◁ **Fishing boats at Mar del Plata** The yellow-and-red boats of the fishermen are lined up along the wharf. The catch of fish includes hake, *corvinas*, and anchovies.

▷ **Gauchos at work on an estancia, or ranch**. Long ago gauchos rode freely through the pampas. Today their work includes branding and tending cattle, and breaking in new horses.

▷ **Beaches at Mar del Plata** There are more than five miles (eight kilometers) of beaches here. In the summer they are always crowded.

Gauchos are tough men who spend the days in harsh sun, rounding up cattle on the pampas, often sleeping outdoors. Traditional gaucho dress is a wide-brimmed hat, pleated pants called *bombachas*, a leather belt, or *rastra*, studded with coins, and high leather boots. Behind his back in his belt, a gaucho tucks his *facón*, a sharp knife and one of his most valued belongings. He also carries a *lazo*, or lasso. Today this has replaced the *boleadoras*, Y-shaped lengths of leather weighted with stones. Gauchos once used boleadoras for catching cattle.

COLONIAL CÓRDOBA

Northwest of Buenos Aires is Córdoba. Argentina's second-largest city is one of the oldest. It is also an important industrial center and home of Argentina's automobile industry. There are many colonial buildings in the city, some are over four hundred years old. These include the cathedral and several churches with fine gold altars and decorated interiors. The country's first university was founded in Córdoba in 1613.

▷ **Yerba mate tree** Warm water is poured onto the leaves to make a tea drink in Córdoba and all over Argentina. Yerba mate plantations are in Argentina's tropical north.

▽ **A railroad network crisscrosses the pampas** Passenger trains for Córdoba used to leave from Belgrano station.

Córdoba is an easy car or bus ride from Buenos Aires. Crossing the flat, endless pampas you will see small villages and large areas planted with wheat and other crops. Everywhere there are herds of cattle.

Visitors often make the journey just to explore the mountains near Córdoba. There are some magnificent views of the hills and lakes. You can see them best if you are walking, hiking, or riding on horseback. There are three ranges of hills: the Sierra Grande, the Sierra Chica, and the Sierra de Comechigones. The highest peak here is Champaqui at 9761 feet (2975 meters).

There are also small villages where colorful music and dance festivals are held. The most important of these festivals is held in Cosquín, 37 miles (60 kilometers) from Córdoba, in January. Villa General Belgrano, a village founded by German immigrants, has an "Oktoberfest" celebration.

On the pampas between Buenos Aires and Córdoba there are many ranches where gaucho festivals are held. In addition to traditional parades, there are noisy rodeos with gauchos demonstrating their riding skills. You will see large barbecues, or *asados*, where whole sides of beef are roasted over charcoal. And at the end of the meal, everybody relaxes with their *mate*, the national drink of Argentina, which is a tea-like drink sipped out of a gourd through a white metal straw.

◁ **Colonial buildings in Córdoba** Carvings, a shield, balconies, and window grilles are typical features of such buildings.

13

BETWEEN THE RIVERS

Several big rivers flow into the Plate River. The two longest are the Paraná River and the Uruguay River, which forms Argentina's border with Uruguay. The name *Entre Rios* means "between rivers." The provinces of Entre Rios, Corrientes, and Misiones lie between these two rivers. The region is known as Mesopotamia.

It was along these rivers that the early Spanish explorer Juan de Solís set off in search of silver. Solís was killed by Indians. Another explorer, Sebastian Cabot, also tried but gave up after three years. An expedition under Pedro de Mendoza followed. Although he too failed to find silver, Mendoza did found the first settlement of Buenos Aires.

Today it is still quite difficult to make a journey upriver, but you may be lucky and get a riverboat up the Paraná.

The fields on either side of the river in Entre Rios are planted with corn and wheat. There are many estancias and great herds of cattle. The largest town on the river is Rosario in the province of Santa Fe. It is more than 200 miles (320 kilometers) north of Buenos Aires. The streets of Rosario are almost as wide as those of the capital, and there are beautiful parks.

The province of Corrientes looks quite different. It is marshy with grass-covered hills and forests. It is a good place to see some interesting wildlife, including the capybara, the world's largest rodent. It is about the size of a pig. The main town is also called Corrientes and is worth a visit at Carnival time before Lent each year. Then the streets are full of music, dancing, and colorful floats.

▷ **The pampas** The coarse grasses that once grew here have been replaced by grasses from Europe to create good pasture. New breeds of cattle have also been introduced.

◁ **Concordia** This is a large prosperous city on the Uruguay River. Nearby, upriver, is the Salto Grande dam.

▽ **The city of Rosario** Many people from abroad came to settle here in the last century.

MISSIONS & FALLS

The Paraná River lies above the town of Corrientes. Sailing a boat through the Alto (Upper) Paraná River is difficult because there are many small islands and rapids. But you can travel by road to Posadas, capital of the province of Misiones. The province was named after Jesuit missions that were settled there in the 1600s. The priests hoped to convert the local Guarani Indians to Christianity.

The Jesuits built missions where the Indians lived and worked, protected from Brazilian slave hunters. Much of the work was farming — growing corn, sugar, and fruit. The Jesuits were the first to grow yerba mate. Many cattle were also kept at the missions. When not working on the farms, the Indians were taught to read and write. They also learned carpentry, weaving, and other useful skills.

The missionaries taught the Indians well, but their success angered other people who preferred to use the Indians as slaves. In the end the Jesuits lost their struggle and were forced to leave in 1767. The missions were deserted and paintings and carvings destroyed. But some interesting ruins have survived. The ruins at San Ignacio Miní, not far from Posadas, are a fine example.

▷ **Posadas on the far bank of the Alto Paraná River** It stands opposite Encarnación in Paraguay. A bridge joins the two towns.

16

◁ **The Iguazú Falls** In the local Indian language *Iguazú* means "great waters." The falls are on the border of Argentina and Brazil.

The Iguazú Falls are a magnificent sight. A series of catwalks leads to the Devil's Throat, the heart of the falls. Every second many tons of water thunder off the rocks into the river below, sending clouds of mist into the air. You can also walk on the bridge below the falls. Be sure to take a raincoat! The area is surrounded by dense rain forest and is a national park.

△ **Ruins of a Jesuit mission** The picture shows a carving on one of the thick sandstone walls of the Jesuit mission at San Ignacio Miní, founded in 1696.

A WILDERNESS

Traveling westward from the Paraná River in northern central Argentina, you come to the region known as the Chaco. It is part of the Gran Chaco that stretches into Brazil, Bolivia, and Paraguay. For a long time the only way across the Chaco was by railroad. Now there are roads, but many are little more than muddy tracks full of holes.

The land is a wilderness of forests, dry thorny scrub, and grasslands dotted with palm trees. A large part of the Chaco lies in the tropics, and some of the highest temperatures in South America have been recorded here. Summer rains also cause heavy flooding.

Chaco in the local language means "hunting ground." There is certainly plenty of wildlife. This includes monkeys, deer, anteaters, armadillos, peccaries (wild pigs), and the tapir, the heaviest animal of the South American forests. There are also snakes, otters, and alligators.

△ **A young Indian woman picking cotton**
Many Indians earn money from seasonal work on the land and in the forest.

18

▷ **Leather from cattle hides** Leather making is one of Argentina's most important industries. Fine leather is made into coats and jackets, bags, shoes, belts, and wallets. Some items sell for high prices in stores in Europe and the United States.

▽ **A fisherman in his boat on the flooded Paraguay River** The fan palms seen in the background are common in the wet parts of the Chaco. The Paraguay River forms part of the border between Paraguay and Argentina.

The forest contains some hardwoods that are very valuable, but trees are also being cut down alarmingly fast to provide charcoal as fuel for local industries. Also, some areas of the forest have been cleared for cattle ranching and farming. Crops such as cotton, corn, sorghum, and sunflowers are grown. The most important tree growing naturally within the forest is the Quebracho, known as the "axbreaker" because it is so hard. Resin, a saplike substance taken from the tree, is used in tanning leather. Other woods are also used to make furniture and hand carvings, which are sold locally.

Some of Argentina's last surviving groups of Indians live in the Chaco, but no one knows exactly how many of them there are. Tribes here include the Toba, Mataco, Mocovi, and Chiriguano. Some still use their native languages. Most now live in much the same way as the other Argentinians do.

19

THE NORTHWEST

The northwest part of Argentina is a fascinating area. There are shiny-white salt lakes with flocks of pink birds called *flamingoes,* dry deserts with tall candlestick-shaped cactus called *cardon,* tropical forests, and snowcapped Andean peaks.

Several of the region's cities, including Tucumán and Salta, are among the oldest in Argentina. They were founded by Spanish settlers making their way south from Peru in the 1500s. Today the cities are a mixture of fine colonial buildings side by side with modern skyscrapers. Do not miss the cathedral in Salta with its magnificent gold altar. Try also to visit the Casa Histórica in Tucumán. This is where Argentina's independence from Spain was declared.

Scientists have discovered signs that there were people living in the region long before the Spaniards arrived. Not far from Tucumán there is a site of carved standing stones, or *menhirs* (totems), that belonged to ancient tribes. In other places there are ruins of stone villages where people were living hundreds of years ago.

The native Indian way of life has survived in the far north of the region. Here people wear colorful traditional dress and make handwoven goods for sale in village markets. One of the prettiest villages to visit is Cachi. It is in the beautiful valley of the Calchaqui River. Cachi has a very old church, much of which is made of cactus wood. Another wonderful trip is on the railroad known as the "train to the clouds." It runs from Salta high into the Andes Mountains.

Tucumán is the center of Argentina's sugar industry. You can visit mills where the cane is made into sugar. Tobacco, red peppers, and cotton are also grown, and there are grape vineyards in many valleys.

▷ **"The Castles" near Salta** This natural rock formation was formed by erosion.

20

▷ **Fruit sellers announce their arrival in the village** They are using a loudspeaker. Horse-drawn carts are widely used in country districts.

△ **Dense forest in a valley near Tucumán** Many valleys are watered by rivers and streams running down from the slopes of the beautiful Andes Mountains.

VINEYARDS & MOUNTAINS

One-fifth of the world's wine comes from Argentina. Most grapes are grown in the "Cuyo," the western region near Argentina's border with Chile. It includes the provinces of Mendoza, San Juan, and San Luis. "Cuyo" means desert land, but water coming down from the Andes irrigates the vineyards here. The industry developed when Europeans arrived in the 1900s. In March the grape harvest is celebrated with a grand festival.

Mendoza has been damaged several times by earthquakes, but is still the largest city in the region. It has prospered not only because of the wine, but also because of its oil, copper, and other minerals. Mendoza has an important place in South American history. From here General San Martín led his "Army of the Andes" over the mountains to free Chile from Spain in 1817. A statue stands in Mendoza in his honor.

Today Mendoza is still the best base for exploring the mountains. The Uspallata Pass is a major route into Chile. But take care — the road climbs to 8,200 feet (2,500 meters). In winter, from July to September, it can be blocked with snow. But it is well worth the effort to see Mount Aconcagua, the highest mountain in the Americas. You will also see a huge Statue of Christ put up to mark the friendship between Chile and Argentina. On the way there is Puente del Inca, a strange natural bridge. There are also many popular ski resorts to visit.

Other important towns in the Cuyo are San Juan and San Luis. This is a mountain region where spices of all kinds are grown. It is also famous for its semi-precious stones, such as agate and lapis.

△ **The Puente del Inca** This natural stone bridge crosses the Mendoza River. It is colored by minerals from the bubbling hot springs beneath it.

▷ **Mount Aconcagua** The mountain was first climbed in 1897 by an expedition led by English climber Edward Fitzgerald. Its name is an Inca word meaning "stone watchtower."

◁ **The guanaco** This animal belongs to the same family as the llama, alpaca, and vicuña. The guanaco is valued for its wool.

LAKE DISTRICT AND A WELSH COMMUNITY

The southern part of Argentina is called Patagonia. It covers about one third of the country and includes part of the island of Tierra del Fuego in the far south. Very few Argentinians live here. Most of Patagonia is empty, windswept plains, but the region also has some of Argentina's most spectacular scenery. Many areas have been made into national parks.

From December to March (Argentina's summer), thousands of tourists set out for the Lake District in the north of Patagonia. The deep-blue lakes are a magnificent sight. They are surrounded by rich green forest and overlooked by snowcapped peaks. The lakes are also good for water sports and for fishing. You will need a permit to fish here. In the winter tourists prefer to go up into the mountains to ski and to climb, starting from towns such as Esquel and Bariloche. Bariloche was settled by Europeans and looks like a mountain town in Switzerland.

Long before the arrival of Europeans, Patagonia was the home of the Mapuches, Patagones, and other Indian tribes. But their lands were colonized, and almost all have disappeared. Among the first European settlers, in 1865, was a group of 150 Welsh people who settled in the Chubut valley. Today some of the community still speak Welsh and hold Welsh cultural festivals.

◁ **Mount Fitzroy in the south of Patagonia** The mountain is 11,000 feet (3,400 meters) high and was not climbed until 1953.

▷ **Sheep ranch in Patagonia** The *paisanos* look after the sheep. Like gauchos, they lead a hard and lonely life.

▷ **Northern Patagonia** From the ski lift visitors get a good view of the Andes Mountains, Bariloche, and the Nahuel Huapi Lake and National Park.

In the remote south of Patagonia, the descendants of early pioneers continue to make their living by running large sheep estancias. But life is changing in Patagonia. Since the discovery of coal and oil there, people and industry have begun to move into the area.

THE WILD SOUTH

Patagonia is wet, windy, and full of wildlife. On the plains you see harelike maras, tiny armadillos, and guanacos. Birds include the partridgelike tinamou, geese, the flamingo, and the flightless rhea, which is similar to an ostrich. Rheas are known as *ñandu* to Argentinians. In the mountains you might see the majestic condor. Along the coast and in the cold Antarctic waters are whales, sea lions, seals, and many penguins.

There are few towns and no cities in Patagonia. The only town with a population of over 100,000 is the port of Comodoro Rivadavia. This town is the center of the region's oil industry. South of Comodoro Rivadavia there is an enormous fossilized forest where trees over 150 million years old are petrified (have become hard like stone). There are also caves with thousand-year-old paintings of hands and animals.

▽ **The Valdés Peninsula wildlife reserve** The tourists are watching a southern right whale.

▽ **A colony of Gentoo Penguins** These are living on islands in the southern Atlantic.

The far south of Patagonia is an icy land, with more sheep ranches. West of the small town of Calafate is the Los Glaciares National Park. At one end of Lake Argentino, in the park, is the Moreno Glacier. From time to time a chunk of the glacier falls into the lake with such a deafening thud that it can be heard miles away.

To the east in the southern Atlantic are the Falkland Islands, known in Argentina as Las Malvinas. The claim to them by both Argentina and Great Britain led to a war in 1982. At the southernmost tip of the South American continent, and at the end of your visit to Argentina, is Cape Horn and the island of Tierra del Fuego. The name Tierra del Fuego means "Land of Fire." The island is separated from the mainland by the Strait of Magellan, a narrow channel named after the famous explorer Ferdinand Magellan, who discovered it in 1520. Argentina and Chile each own part of the island.

▽ **The town of Ushuaia, overlooking the Beagle Channel** Ushuaia is the southernmost town in the entire world.

ARGENTINA FACTS AND FIGURES

People

Most Argentinians are descended from Europeans who arrived in the 1700s and 1800s. Settlers came from Spain, Italy, Germany, Britain, and Switzerland. In some communities the culture and traditions of these peoples have remained strong.

Few of the native Indian tribes have survived. In the northwest, where Spanish-Indian marriages took place, there is a small number of people who are part Spanish and part Indian. These people are called "mestizos."

△ **A gaucho working leather to make a pair of boots** Gauchos still use leather for their saddles, lassoes, and other gear.

Trade and Industry

Cattle and sheep have for a long time been the core of Argentina's industry. They provide the raw materials not only for skins and hides, but for canned meat such as corned beef. Processed food and drink are an important part of Argentina's manufacturing industry. Production has greatly increased since the 1960s, when more land was put aside for crops.

The country has large forests, but the timber industry is not up to date. Hardwood trees are the most valuable.

Argentinian factories make goods such as refrigerators, television sets, cars, and ships, as well as paper, machinery of all kinds, and electrical equipment.

Argentina has almost all the oil it needs. All of it comes from offshore fields. There are also gas reserves, although at present much of Argentina's gas is brought in from Bolivia. The rivers are a good source of hydroelectric power. Mineral deposits include copper, lead, zinc, tin, gold, silver, and uranium.

Fishing

Argentina has a long coastline but its fishing industry is small. People prefer to eat meat. Seafish include hake, anchovies, shark, and *corvina*. Salmon and trout are found in the Lake District and in rivers in the south. Dorado are well known in the north. Other river fish include eel, catfish, and piranha.

Farming

Agriculture in Argentina is centered on the pampas grassland, with its fertile soil and good climate. The number of cattle has decreased in recent years because of competition from other meat-exporting countries such as Brazil and the European countries. As a result, more wheat and cereals are being grown on the pampas.

Argentina's other crops include corn, sorghum, tea, tobacco, rice, and sugarcane. It is the world's third-largest producer of soya and fifth-largest producer of wine. Fruit is also grown in many of the subtropical valleys.

Sheep farming is extensive in Patagonia, and Argentina is a leading exporter of wool.

Food

The favorite food in Argentina is steak or *bife*. It is cooked in restaurants on grills, or *parrillas*. It can be served alone as *bife de costilla* (like T-bone steak) or as *bife de chorizo* (fillet steak). A *parrillada* is a mixed grill of steak served with other meats, such as kidneys and sausage. Restaurants also offer pork, lamb, and other meats, but none are as popular as beef.

Other dishes include thick stews, such as *locro* made of corn, white beans, beef, sausage, pumpkin, and herbs. Chicken is eaten with a variety of vegetables and rice.

Food from other countries, such as Italian pizzas and pasta, are available almost everywhere.

Schools

By law, all children aged six to fourteen have to go to school. They attend at primary and secondary level. Some do not complete their education as they may be needed to work at home or because school is too far away. Most town schools are better equipped than those in rural areas.

△ **The maned wolf** There are no true wolves in South America. The maned wolf is a close relative of the fox and dog. It lives in open grasslands and dry forests.

Pupils have lessons in science, mathematics, and other subjects similar to those in other parts of the world. Over half a million students go on to a university. More than 95 percent of Argentinians can read and write.

The Media

Daily newspapers in Buenos Aires include *La Nación*, *Clarín*, *La Prensa*, and *Ambito Financiero*. The *Buenos Aires Herald* is published in English and *Le Quotidien* in French. Many towns have local newspapers.

Magazines on a wide variety of topics, such as politics, women's and children's interests, and computers, are published.

Argentina has many TV and radio stations. Buenos Aires has five TV channels. About 80 percent of the population has access to a TV set and 90 percent to a radio.

Art and Literature

Among Argentina's best-known twentieth-century artists are Antonio Berni and Raquel Forner. Their work shows the influence of European styles.

Argentina's most famous writer, Jorge Luis Borges, died in 1986. His work has been translated into many languages.

Music

The tango is the dance music most associated with Argentina. Tango music is played on many instruments, but especially on the *bandoneon*, a relative of the accordion. Performers from all over the world perform at the Colón Theater in Buenos Aires.

Argentina's leading composer, Alberto Ginastera, composed many operas. He died in 1983.

ARGENTINA FACTS AND FIGURES

Religion

More than 90 percent of Argentinians are Roman Catholics. Christianity was brought to Argentina by Spanish priests and missionaries in the 1500s.

The president and vice-president must be Roman Catholics by law. People may practice the religion of their choice. Religion is not taught in all state schools.

Indian peoples and mestizos of the northwest have also kept some old spiritual beliefs.

Festivals and Holidays

The following are national holidays in Argentina:

January 1 **New Year's Day**
May 1 **Labor Day**
May 25 **Anniversary of the May Revolution**
June 10 **Malvinas Day** To commemorate the Falklands War
Jun 20 **Flag Day**
July 9 **Independence Day**
August 17 **Anniversary of the death of General San Martín**
October 12 **Columbus Day**
November 10 **Día de la Tradición** Follows days of gaucho parades throughout Argentina
December 25 **Christmas Day**

△ **An Argentine soccer fan** Her face is painted in the national colors. Argentina won the World Soccer Championships in 1978 and 1986.

Sports

Argentina's favorite sport is *futbol*, or soccer, and it has won the World Cup twice.

Argentinians excel in polo, horse show jumping, rugby, hockey, and boxing. The great Argentinian sportsman Juan Fangio, the Grand Prix racing driver, won the championship five times in the 1950s.

The sport of *pato* originated in Argentina. The game has four players, a leather ball with handles, and is like basketball on horseback.

Plants

Within the forests near Córdoba, the algarrobo tree is highly valued. It provides fruit, wood for fence posts, and firewood. A plant native to the pampas, the *ombú*, gives welcome shade to gauchos and cattle. Tall grasses and large thistles also grow on the pampas. In southern Argentina are the Alerces, giant evergreens that grow very tall.

In its variety of rain and cloud forests, Argentina has palms, pines, and many beautiful flowering trees such as the Jacaranda and Tabebuia.

Animals

Jaguars, anteaters, monkeys, armadillos, and sloths all live in the forests. Whales, seals, and penguins are found on the coasts, and on the pampas there are foxes, deer, and rodents.

Some of Argentina's unusual species of birds are the black-necked swan, the huge Andean condor, the spectacular Magellanic woodpecker, and the hornero, or ovenbird. Birds such as toucans, parrots, and hummingbirds live in the tropical forests.

HISTORY

The first people to settle in Argentina arrived from Asia, crossing the Bering Strait and moving down through North America during the Ice Age, about 10,000 B.C. They lived by hunting, fishing, and farming.

In 1516 Juan de Solís was the first European to sail up the Plate River. During the 1500s Spanish treasure-hunters arrived in western Argentina and founded towns there. Buenos Aires was founded later.

Argentina was a Spanish colony for almost 300 years. For over 200 years it was ruled from Peru, and the western towns prospered. Buenos Aires did not become the capital until 1776. Then tradesmen from the new capital decided to fight for their independence from Spain. General José de San Martín led Argentina to freedom in 1816.

From 1829 until 1852 the country was ruled by the ruthless dictator Juan Manuel Rosas. In 1862 President Bartolomé Mitre started some social reforms, built schools, and encouraged the building of railroads. Immigrants arrived to help open up the pampas. By the end of the 1800s the country was quite prosperous.

The most famous president of this century, Juan Perón, worked with his wife, Eva, to help the poor. But in 1976 a group of generals seized power. During their rule thousands of people died or disappeared. These generals were also responsible for the war with Great Britain over the Falkland Islands. Today Argentina has a democratically elected government.

LANGUAGE

The majority of Argentinians speak Spanish, which is the official language. But there are different dialects, which a European Spanish speaker may find difficult to understand.

Some of the people who have settled in Argentina, such as the Italians, have introduced new words into the language. There are also communities who use only their original language among themselves.

Only a small number of Indian groups still speak their native languages.

Useful words and phrases

English	Spanish
One	uno
Two	dos
Three	tres
Four	cuatro
Five	cinco
Six	seis
Seven	siete
Eight	ocho
Nine	nueve
Ten	diez
Sunday	domingo
Monday	lunes
Tuesday	martes
Wednesday	miércoles

Useful words and phrases

English	Spanish
Thursday	jueves
Friday	viernes
Saturday	sábado
Excuse me	Perdóneme
Good morning	Buenos días
Good night	Buenos noches
Good-bye	Adiós
Very good	Muy bien
Please	Por favor
Thank you	Muchas gracias
Yes	Sí
No	No
Can you speak English?	¿Habla usted Inglés?

INDEX

Acknowledgments
Book created for Highlights for Children, Inc. by Bender Richardson White.
Editors: Peter MacDonald and Lionel Bender
Designer: Malcolm Smythe
Art Editor: Ben White
Editorial Assistant: Madeleine Samuel
Picture Researcher: Madeleine Samuel
Production: Kim Richardson

Maps produced by Oxford Cartographers, England.
Banknotes from Thomas Cook Currency Services.
Stamps from Stanley Gibbons.

Editorial Consultant: Andrew Gutelle
Guide to Argentina is approved by The Argentine Consulate General, London
Argentina Consultant: Ruth Mehl, Buenos Aires, Argentina
Managing Editor, Highlights New Products: Margie Hayes Richmond

Picture Credits
DS = David Simson/DAS Photos. SAP = South American Pictures/Tony Morrison.
t = top, b = bottom, r = right, l= left, c = center.
Cover: SAP/Tony Morrison. Page 6: SAP/Tony Morrison. 6-7: DS. 7: SAP/Tony Morrison. 8t: SAP/Chris Sharp. 8-9: SAP. 9t: DS. 10: SAP/Frank Nowikowski. 11t: DS. 11b: SAP/Tony Morrison. 12: SAP/Tony Morrison. 13t: SAP/Tony Morrison. 13b:DS. 14: SAP/Tony Morrison. 15t: SAP/Tony Morrison. 15b: DS. 16-17t, 16-17b: SAP/Tony Morrison. 17r: DS. 18l: SAP/Chris Sharp. 18-19: SAP/Tony Morrison. 19t: SAP/Chris Sharp. 20-21: ZEFA Photos. 21t, 21b: SAP/Tony Morrison. 22: SAP/Chris Sharp. 23t, 23b: SAP/Frank Nowikowski. 24: ZEFA/Hecker. 25t: ZEFA/Abril. 25b: SAP/David Horwell. 26l: SAP/Frank Nowikowski. 26r: SAP/Marion Morrison. 27: SAP/Hilary Bradt. 28: SAP/Chris Sharp. 29: SAP/Tony Morrison. 30: SAP/Frank Nowikowski.